ALFRED's
SACRED PERFORMER
WORSHIP SUITES

Late Int

MW01011919

THE COMPLETE WORSHIP SUITES

18 *Expressive Suites Arranged for Solo Piano*
Correlated with Scriptural Themes

Alfred Music Publishing Co., Inc.
P.O. Box 10003
Van Nuys, CA 91410-0003
alfred.com

ISBN-10: 0-7390-6509-2
ISBN-13: 978-0-7390-6509-9

FOREWORD

The Complete Worship Suites includes 18 expressive suites arranged for late intermediate to advanced pianists. 17 of today's top arrangers of Christian music are represented in this collection, each adding a unique interpretation and style to the most familiar and best-loved sacred works:

- Cindy Berry
- Shirley Brendlinger
- Larry Dalton
- Marilynn Ham
- Mark Hayes
- Matt Hyzer
- Bernadine Johnson
- Victor Labenske
- Martha Mier
- Anna Laura Page
- Kenon D. Renfrow
- Mary K. Sallee
- Jan Sanborn
- Myra Schubert
- Mike Springer
- Robert D. Vandall
- Kim Williams

Each inspiring suite consists of three to four pieces and sometimes a medley, all united by a timeless spiritual theme that is supported by correlating Scripture verses. The pieces can serve as prelude, offertory, and postlude when played at a religious service, or may be played in full as a suite for a longer performance setting. To assist in planning, approximate performance times are included for each piece.

CONTENTS

HOLINESS

I. Love Divine, All Loves Excelling

*This is love: not that we loved God, but that He loved us, and sent
His son to be the atoning sacrifice for our sins.*
—I John 4:10

John Zundel
Arr. Victor Labenske

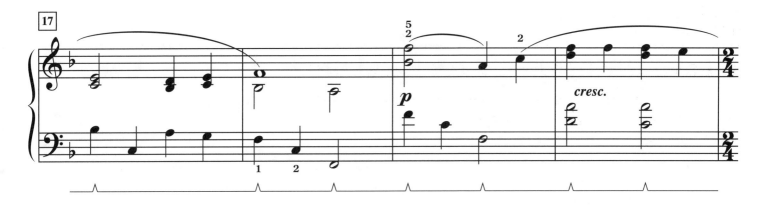

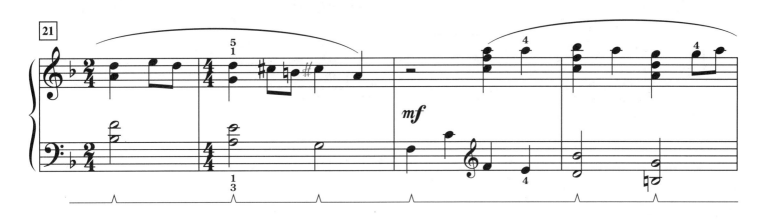

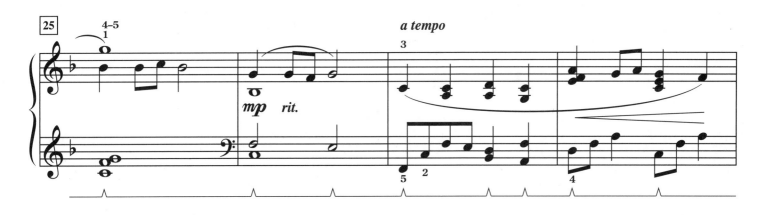

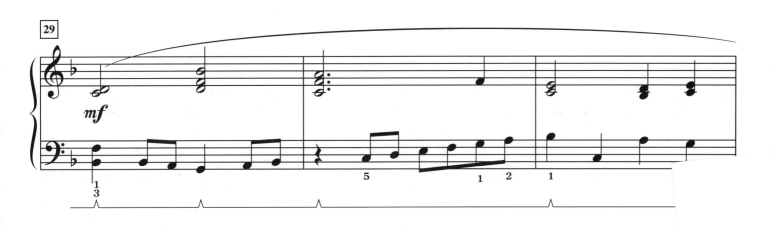

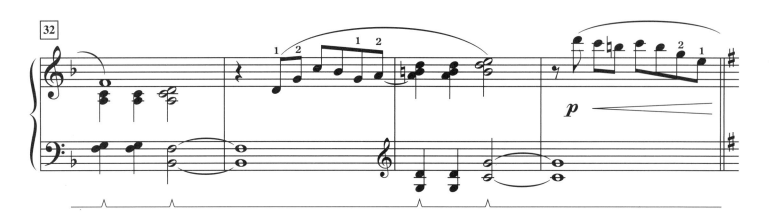

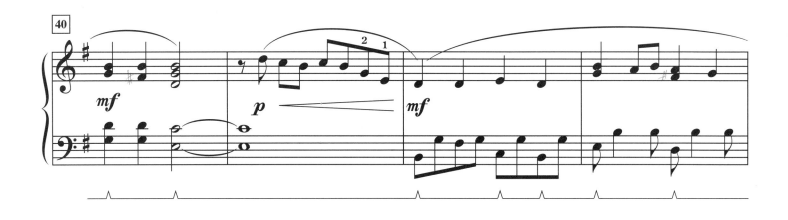
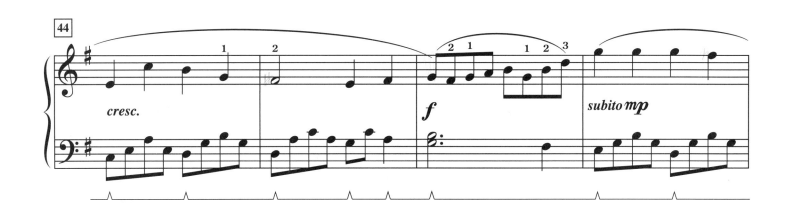

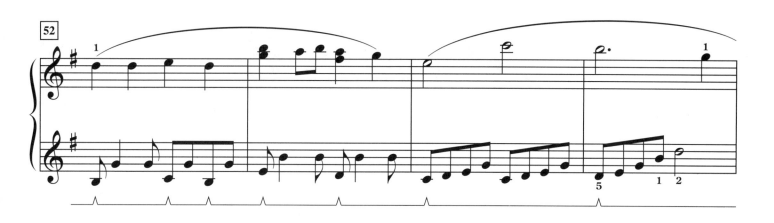

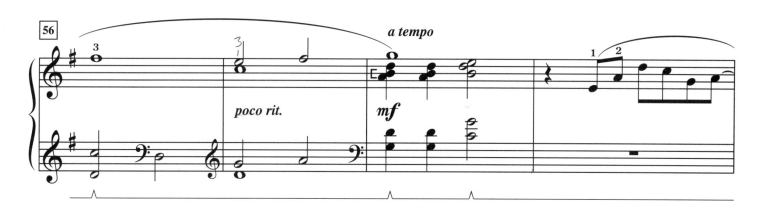

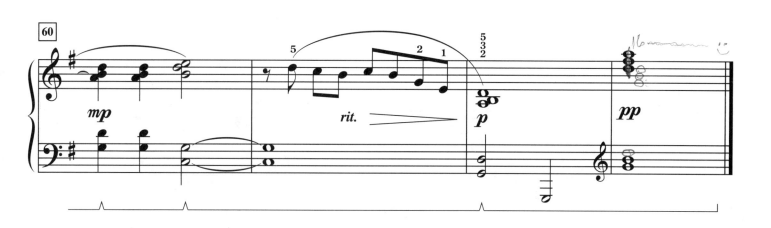

II. O to Be Like Thee

I want to know Christ, and the power of His resurrection, and the fellowship of His sufferings,
being made like Him in His death, so that I might attain to the resurrection from the dead.
—Philippians 3:10

William J. Kirkpatrick
Arr. Victor Labenske

III. Spirit of God, Descend upon My Heart

Even on my servants, men and women alike, I will pour out my Spirit in those days.
—Joel 2:29

Frederick C. Atkinson
Arr. Victor Labenske

FELLOWSHIP WITH GOD

I. Nearer, My God, to Thee

Come near to God, and He will come near to you.
—James 4:8

Music by Lowell Mason
Arr. Martha Mier

II. Be Thou My Vision

Let us fix our eyes on Jesus, the author and perfector of our faith,
who for the joy set before Him endured the cross, scorning the shame,
and sat down at the right hand of the throne of God.
    —Hebrews 12:2

Traditional Irish Melody
Arr. Martha Mier

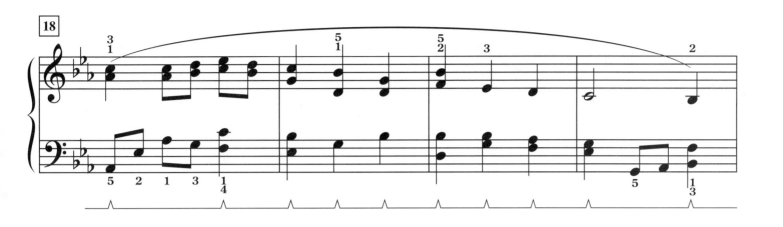

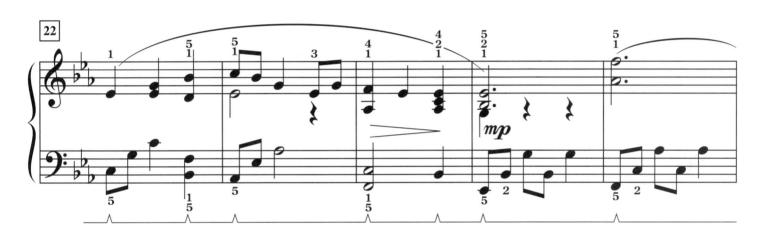

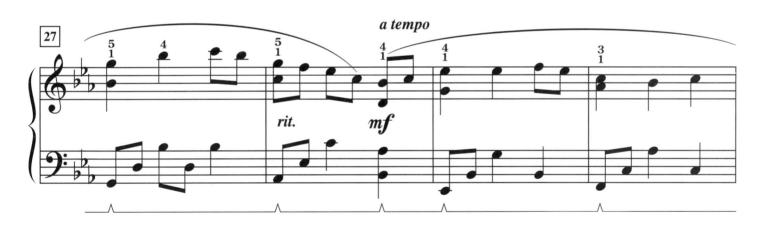

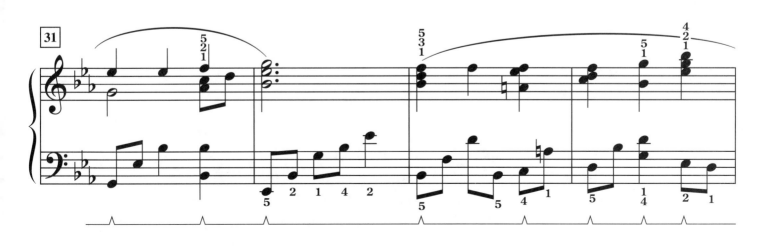

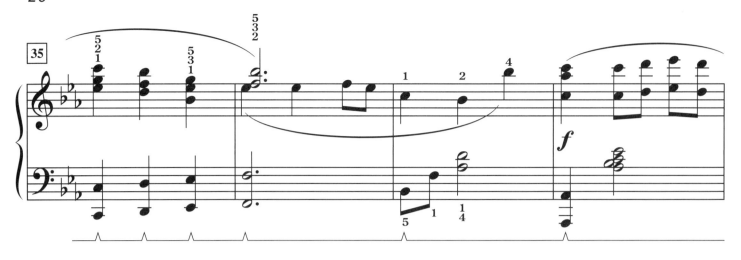

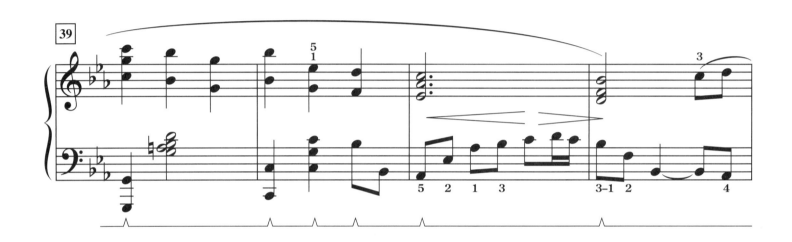

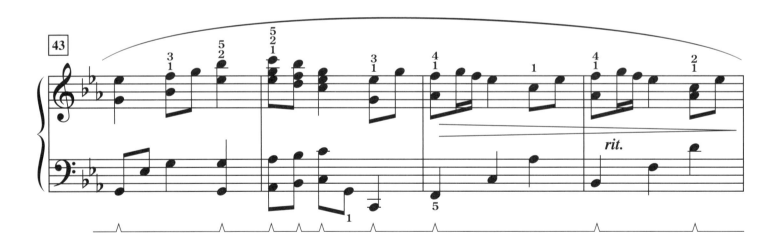

III. I Want Jesus to Walk with Me

When Jesus spoke again to the people, he said, "I am the light of the world.
Whoever follows me will never walk in darkness, but will have the light of life."
   —John 8:12

Spiritual
Arr. Martha Mier

Moderately fast

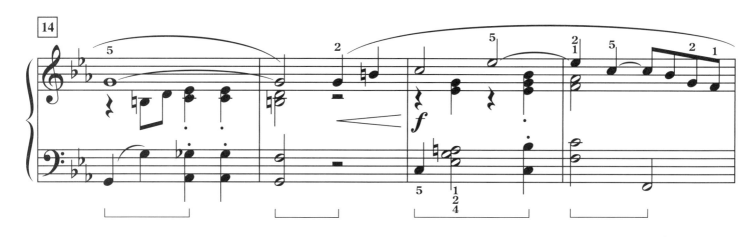

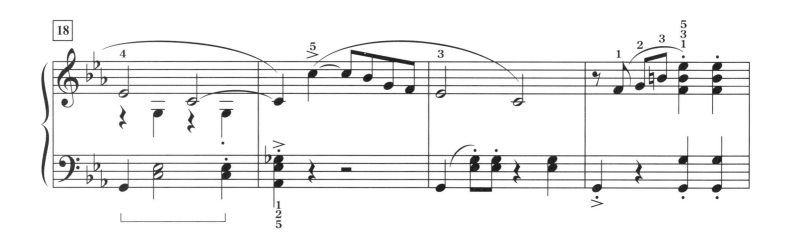

HEAVENLY BLESSINGS

I. Come Thou Fount of Every Blessing

*Then the angel showed me the river of the water of life, as clear
as crystal, flowing from the throne of God and of the Lamb...*
—Revelation 22:1

John Wyeth
Arr. Cindy Berry

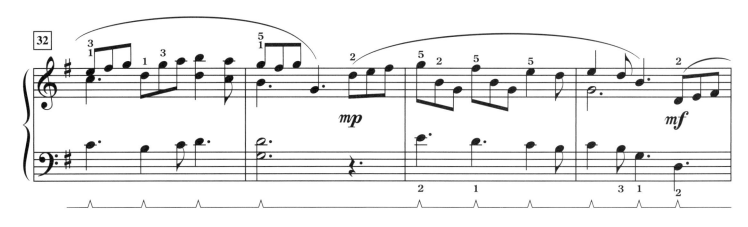

II. Amazing Grace

For the wages of sin is death, but the gift of God is eternal life in Jesus Christ our Lord.
  —Romans 6:23

Early American folk melody
Arr. Cindy Berry

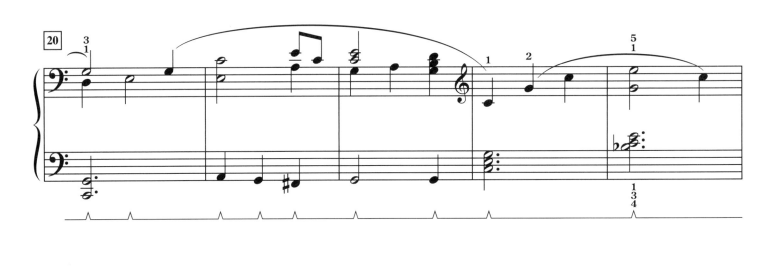

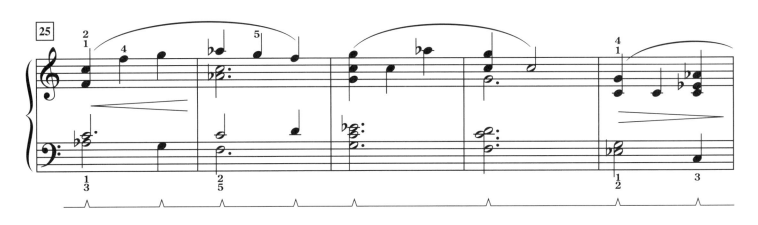

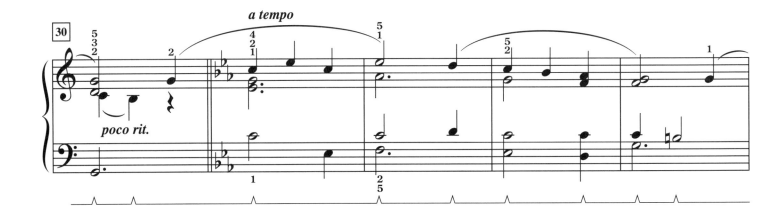

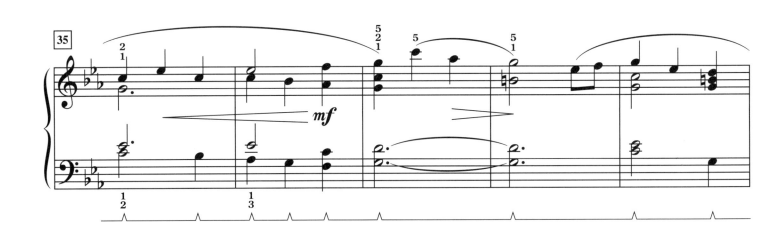

III. On Jordan's Stormy Banks I Stand

The righteous will inherit the land and dwell in it forever.
  —Psalm 37:29

Traditional American melody
Arr. Cindy Berry

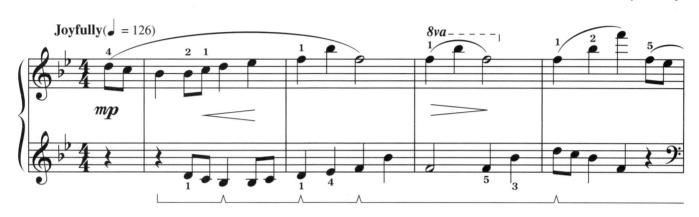

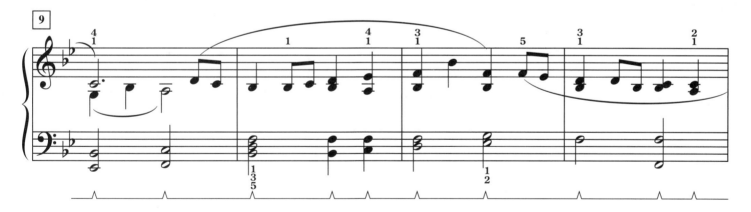

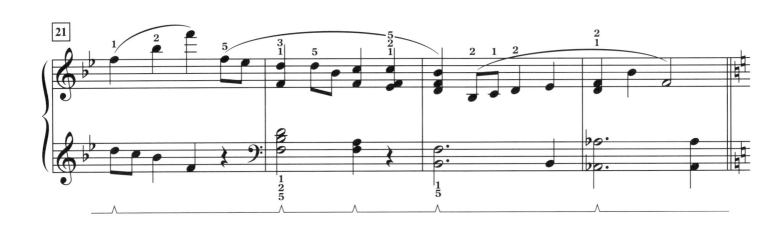

(Approx. Performance Time—3:00)

JOY AND ASSURANCE

I. Blessed Assurance

For I am convinced that nothing can ever separate us from His love.
—Romans 8:38, 39

Phoebe P. Knapp
Arr. Jan Sanborn

* roll if necessary

* roll if necessary

II. I Will Sing the Wondrous Story

Eternal life is in Him, and this life gives light to all mankind.
   —John 1:4

Peter P. Billhorn
Arr. Jan Sanborn

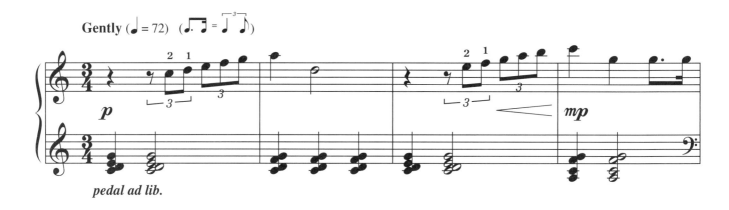

III. My Redeemer

I will praise You with music, telling of Your faithfulness to all Your promises.
—Psalm 71:22, 23

James McGranahan
Arr. Jan Sanborn

HOLY COMMUNION—A VIEW OF THE CROSS

*Let us fix our eyes on Jesus, the author and perfecter of our faith,
who for the joy set before him endured the cross, scorning its shame,
and sat down at the right hand of the throne of God.*
    —Hebrews 12:2 (NIV)

I. At the Cross—Ralph E. Hudson
II. Beneath the Cross of Jesus—Frederick C. Maker
III. In the Cross of Christ I Glory—Ithamar Conkey
Arr. Marilynn Ham

First Movement:
At the Cross
(Approx. Time – 2:45)

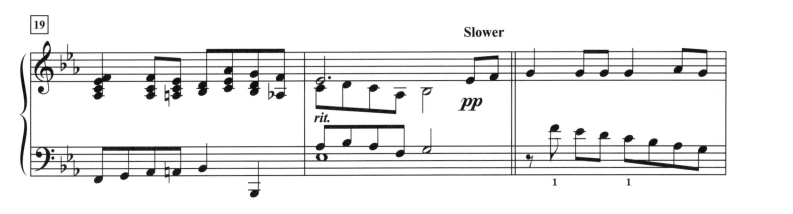

Second Movement:
Beneath the Cross of Jesus
(Approx. Time – 2:30)

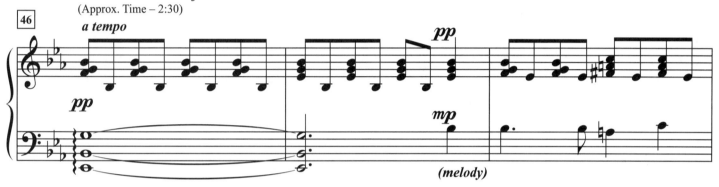

ⓐ To conclude the first movement, end at measure 45. To continue into the second movement, go from measure 44 directly to measure 46.

48

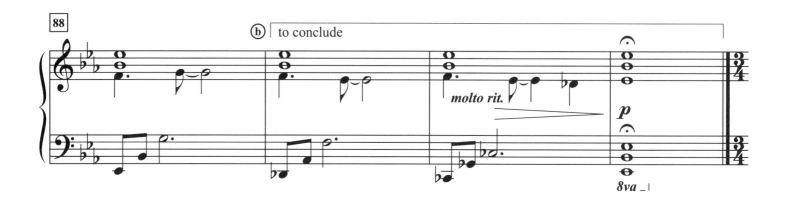

Third Movement:
In the Cross of Christ I Glory
(Approx. Time – 2:30)

Slower, with dignity

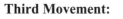 To conclude the second movement, end at measure 91. To continue into
the third movement, go from measure 88 directly to measure 92.

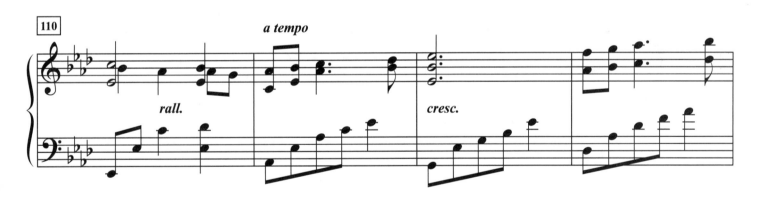

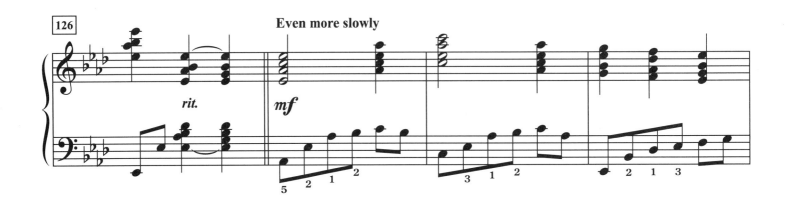

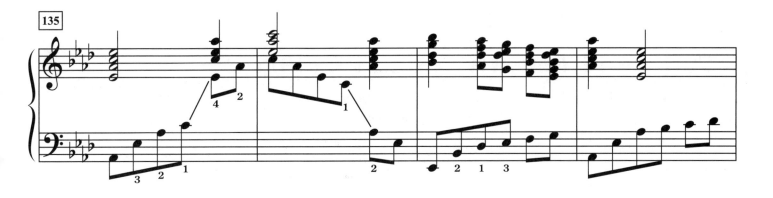

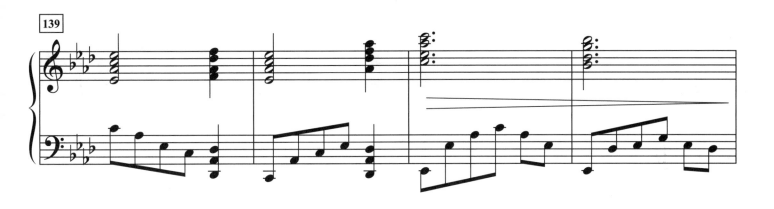

HEAVEN, OUR HOME

I. Softly and Tenderly Jesus Is Calling

*I tell you that in the same way there will be more rejoicing in heaven over one sinner
who repents than over ninety-nine righteous persons who do not need to repent.*
—Luke 15:7 (NIV)

Will L. Thompson
Arr. Robert D. Vandall

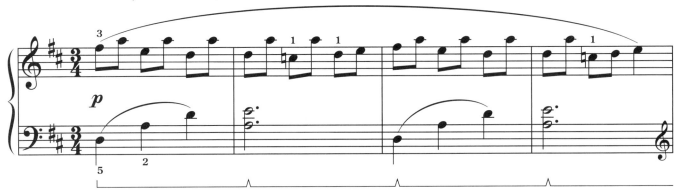

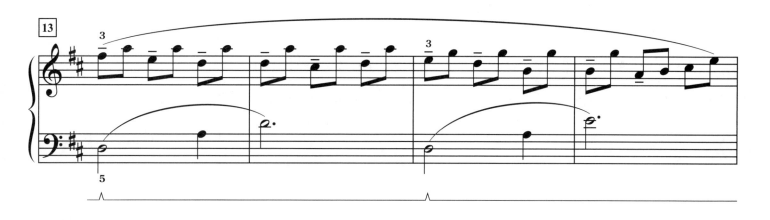

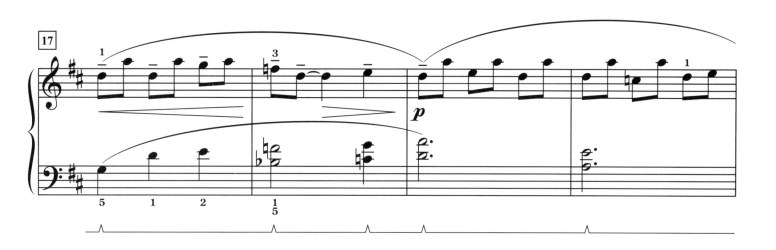

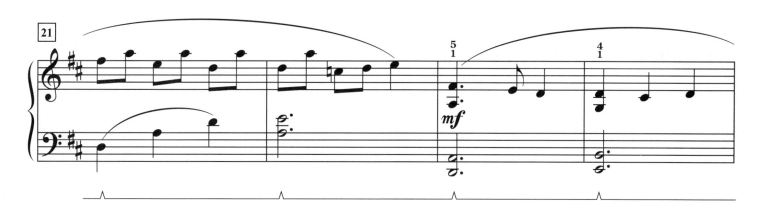

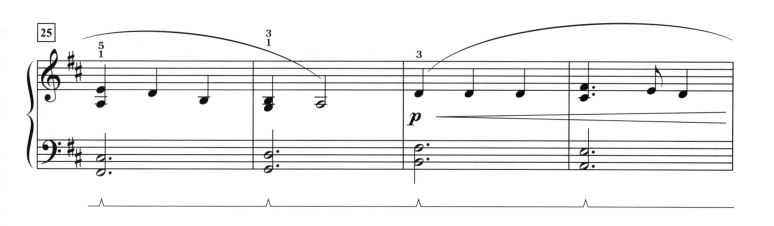

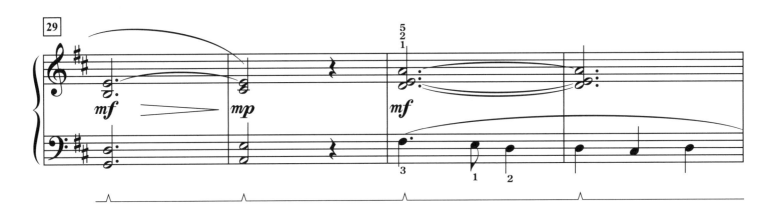

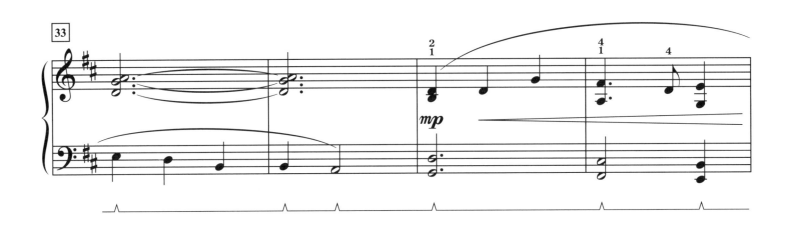

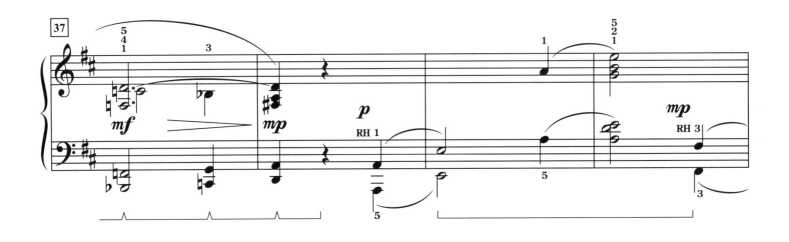

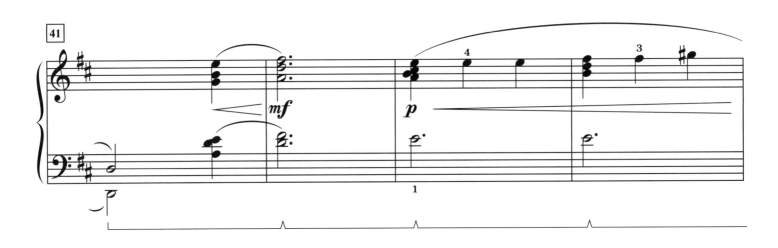

II. Swing Low, Sweet Chariot

*And if I go and prepare a place for you, I will come back and
take you to be with me that you also may be where I am.*
   —John 14:3 (NIV)

Spiritual
Arr. Robert D. Vandall

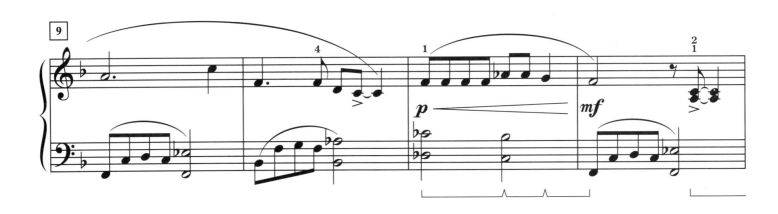

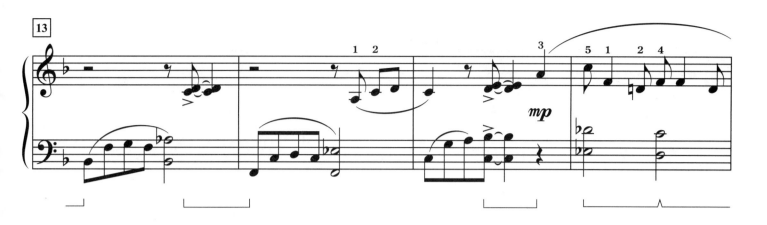

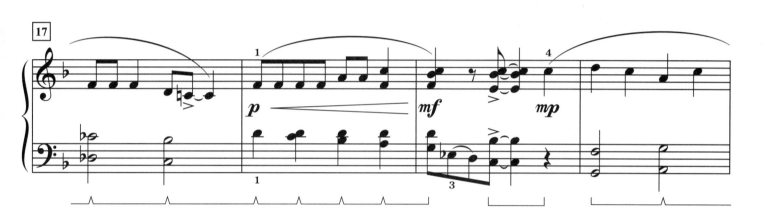

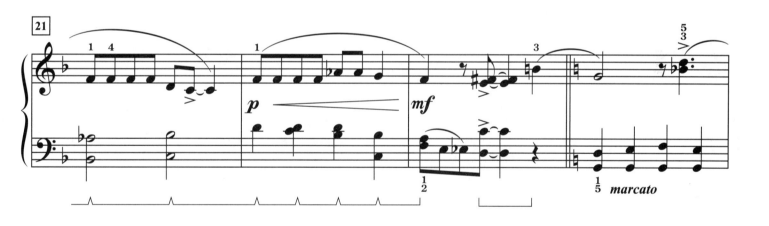

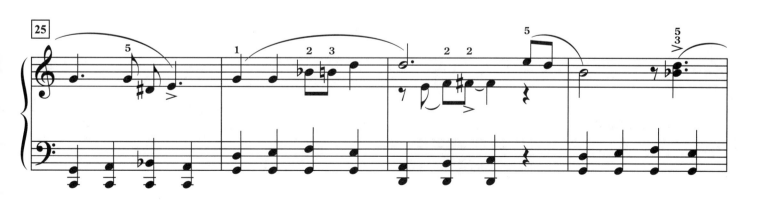

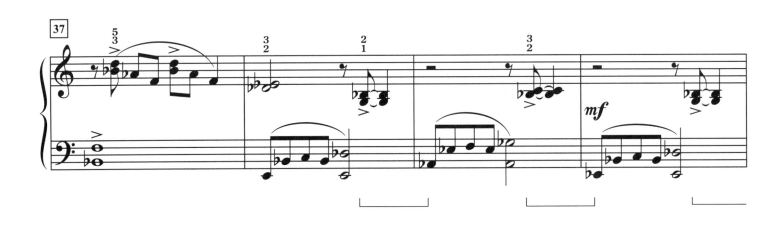

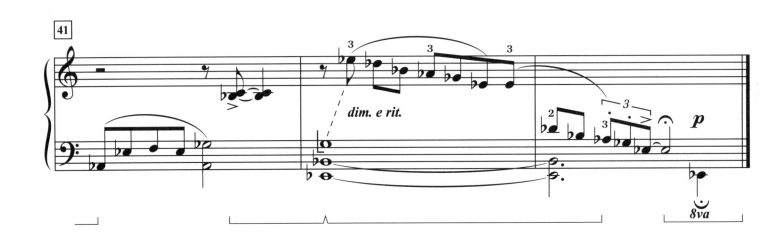

III. In the Sweet Bye and Bye

Set your minds on things above, not on earthly things.
    —Colossians 3:2 (NIV)

Joseph P. Webster
Arr. Robert D. Vandall

Moderately slow, with expression and freedom (♩ = ca. 80)

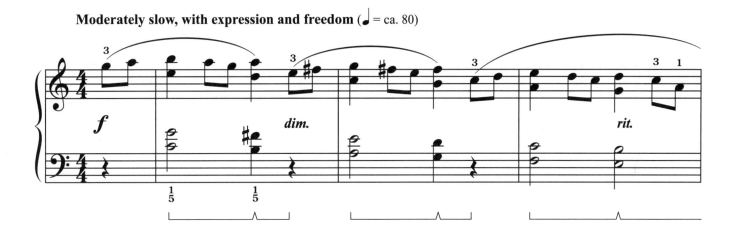

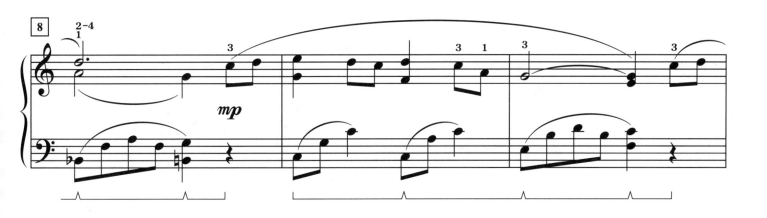

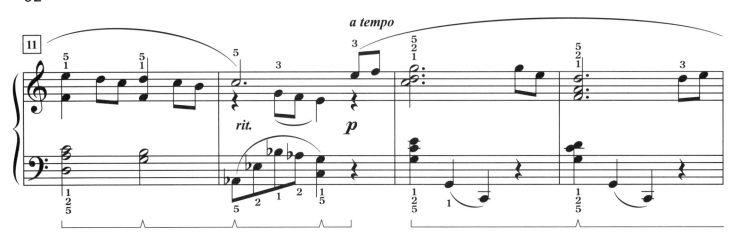

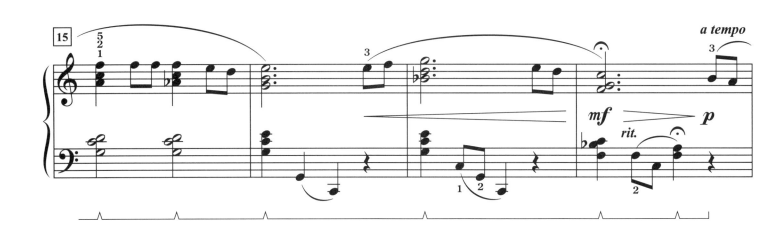

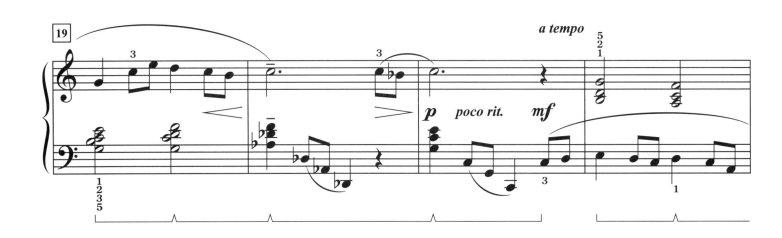

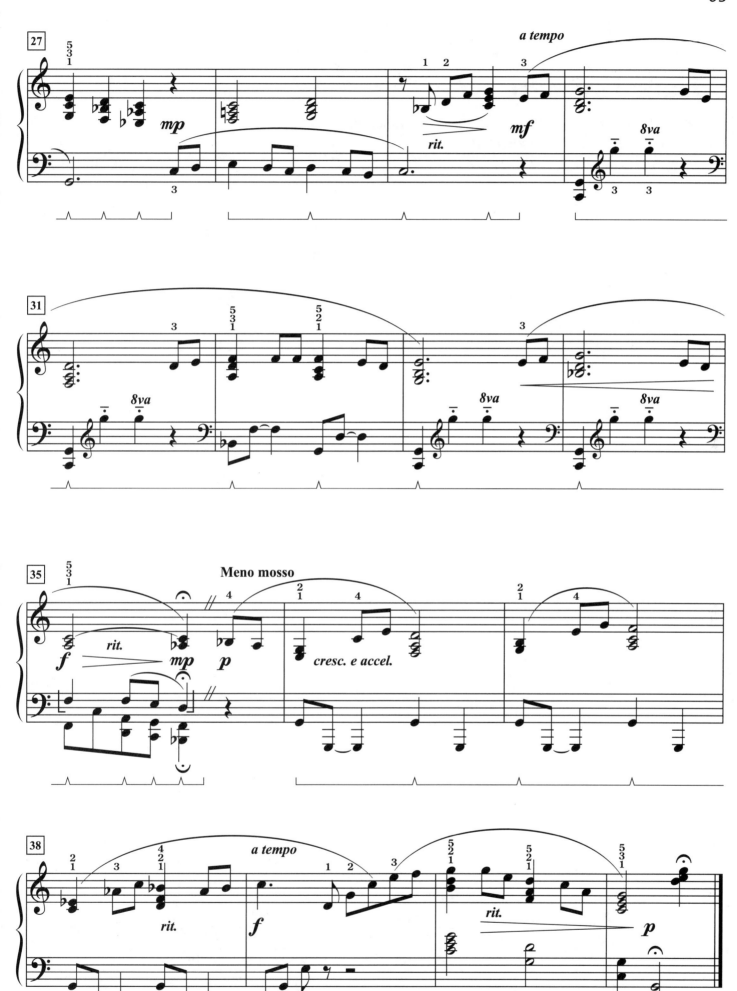

JESUS CHRIST, FRIEND AND SAVIOR

I. Jesus Loves Me

Let the little children come to me and do not hinder them,
for the Kingdom of God belongs to such as these.
—Mark 10:14

William B. Bradbury
Arr. Kim Williams

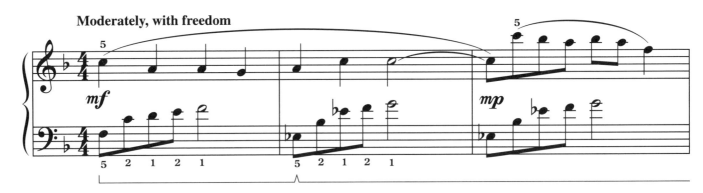

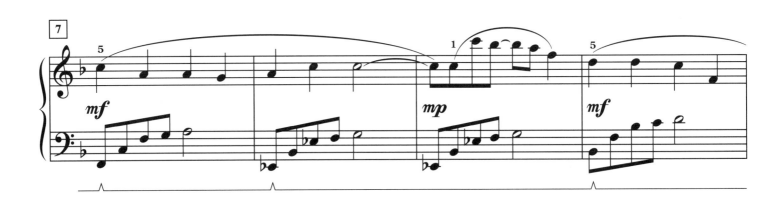

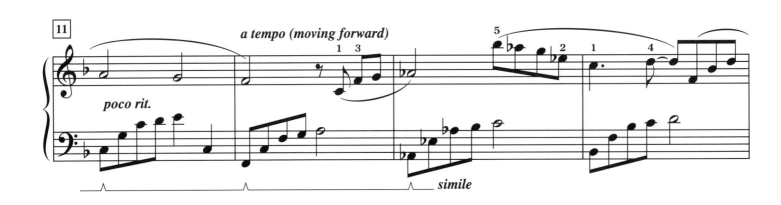

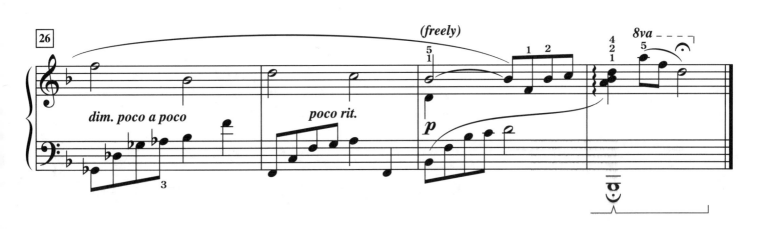

II. What a Friend We Have in Jesus

Cast all your cares upon Him, because He cares for you.
   —I Peter 5:7

Charles C. Converse
Arr. Kim Williams

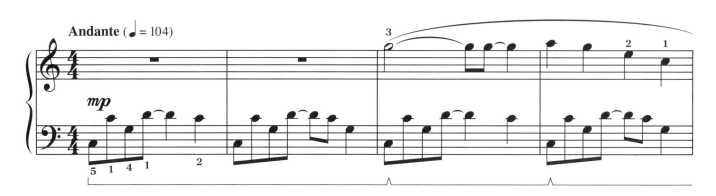

III. Jesus Is All the World to Me

How awesome is the Lord most high, the great King over all the earth.
—Psalms 47:2

Will L. Thompson
Arr. Kim Williams

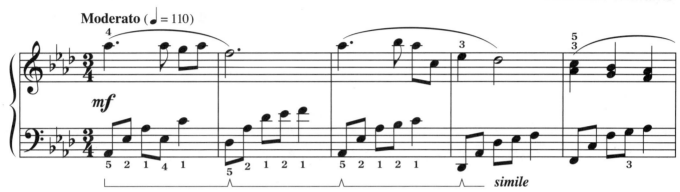

IV. Stand Up, Stand Up for Jesus

Jesus Christ is the same yesterday and today and forever.
    —Hebrews 13:8

Adam Geibel
Arr. Kim Williams

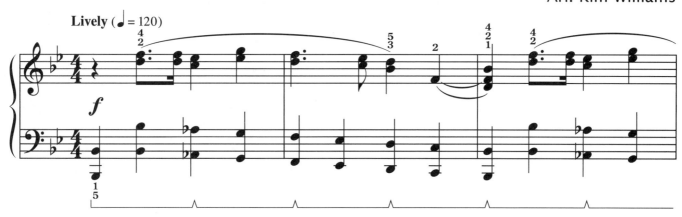

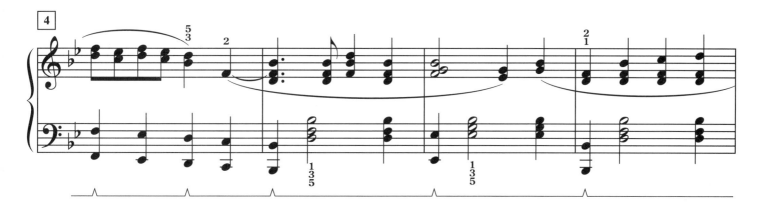

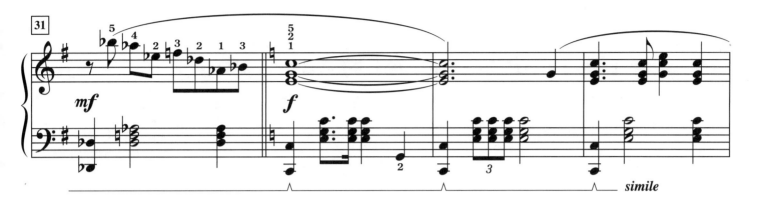

PRAISE HIM!

I. Praise the Lord! Ye Heavens, Adore Him

It is good to praise the Lord and make music to Your name, O Most High.
—Psalm 92:1

Rowland H. Prichard
Arr. Mike Springer

II. Praise to the Lord, the Almighty

Praise the Lord, all His works everywhere in His dominion. Praise the Lord, O my soul.
—Psalm 103:22

William Bennett
Arr. Mike Springer

III. Praise Him! Praise Him!

I will praise You with music, telling of Your faithfulness to all Your promises.
    —Psalm 71:22, 23

Chester G. Allen
Arr. Mike Springer

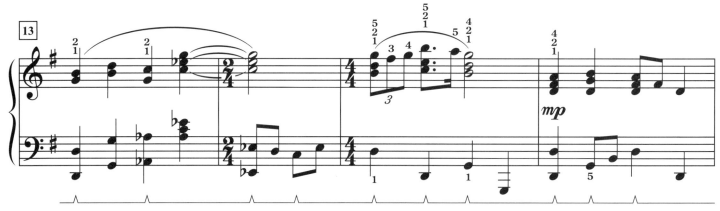

More relaxed

With grandeur

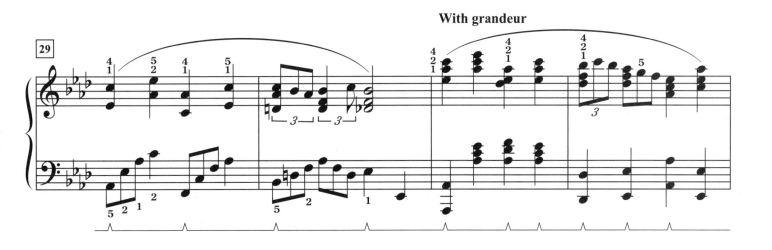

COMFORT IN THE TIME OF NEED

I. It Is Well with My Soul

For I am convinced that nothing can ever separate us from His love.
    —Romans 8:38, 39

Philip P. Bliss
Arr. Mary K. Sallee

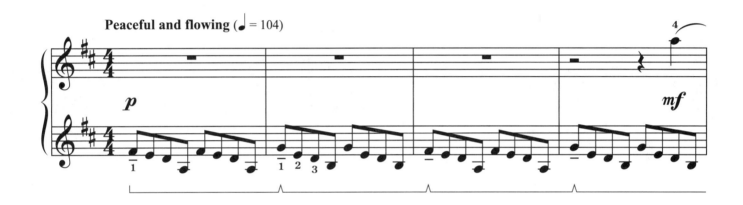

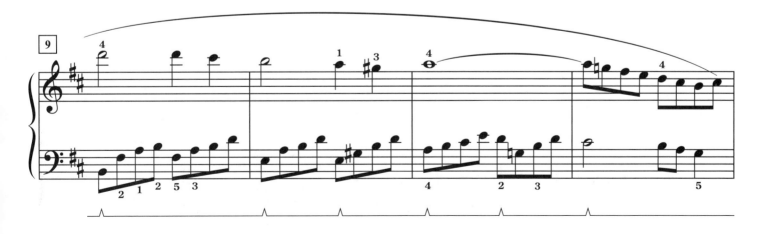

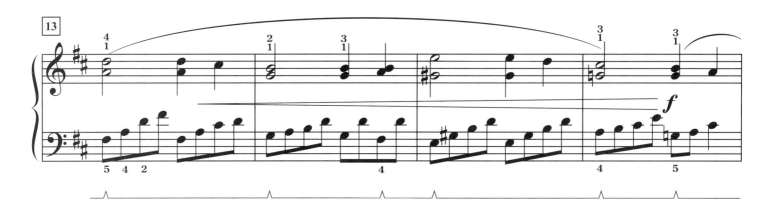

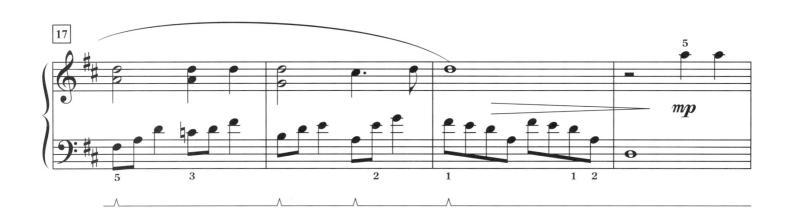

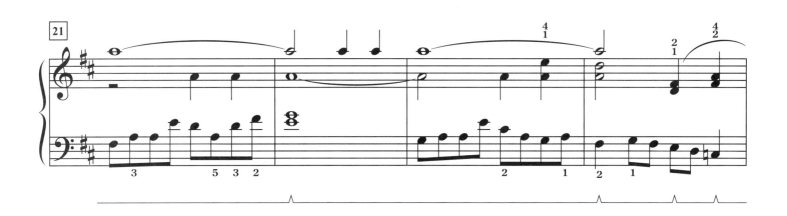

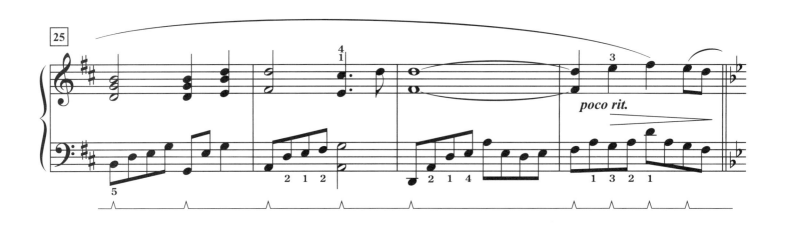

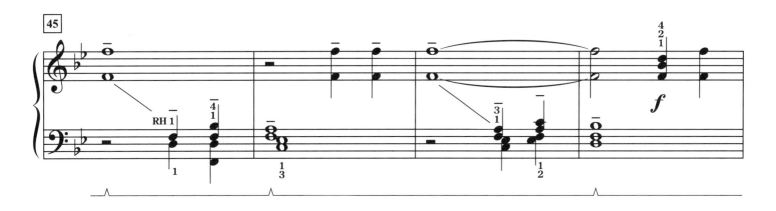

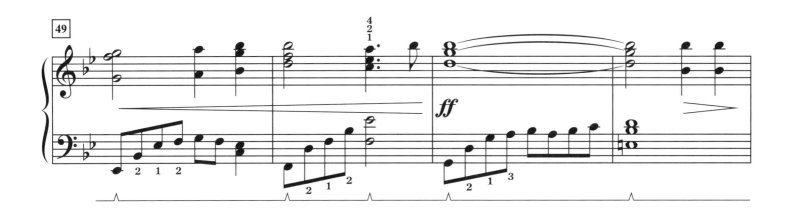

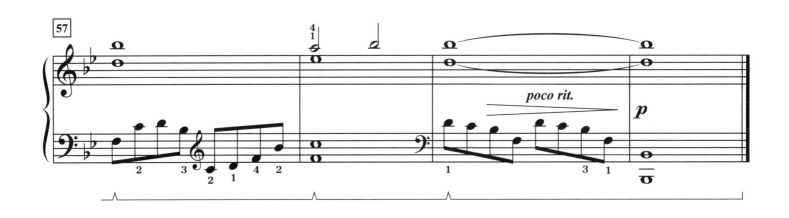

II. There Is a Balm in Gilead

Eternal life is in Him, and this life gives light to all mankind.
        —John 1:4

Spiritual
Arr. Mary K. Sallee

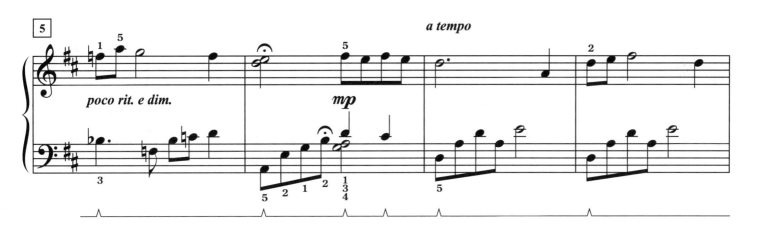

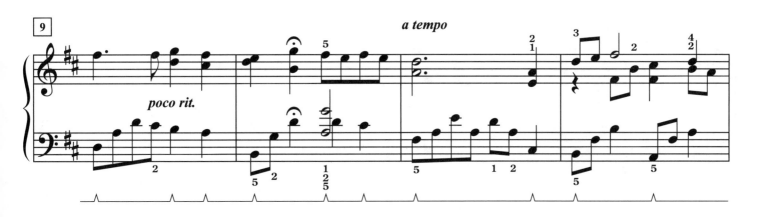

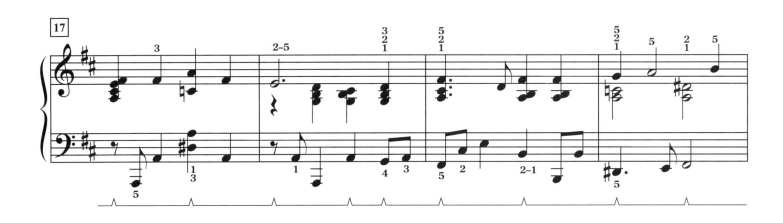

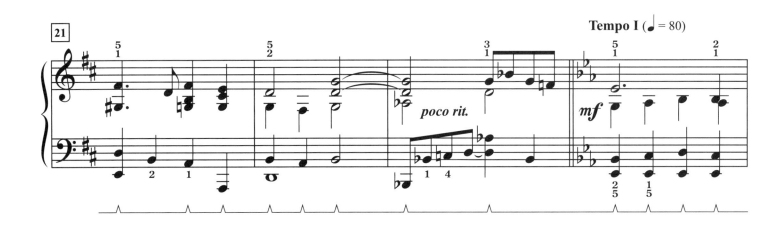

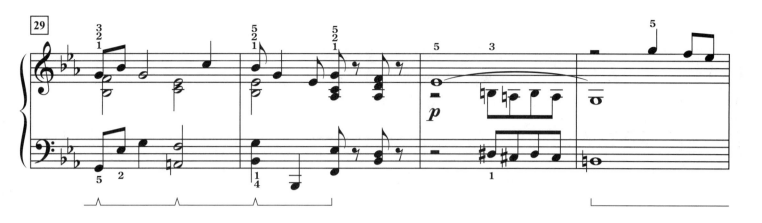

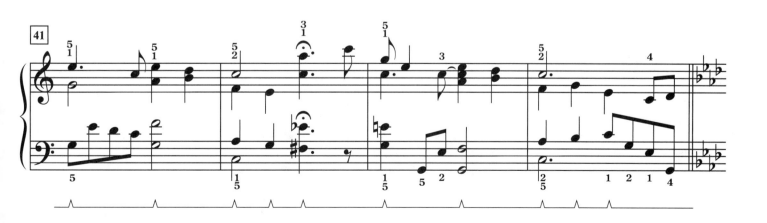

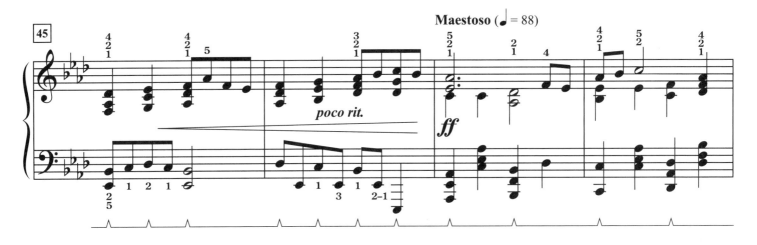

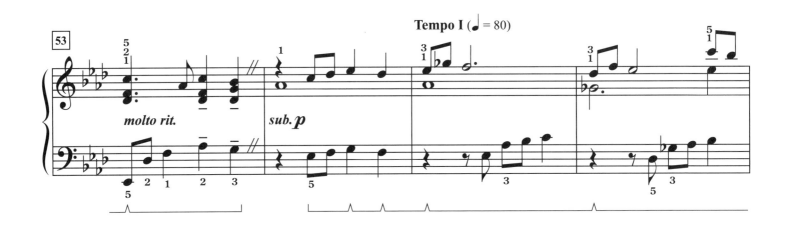

III. In the Garden

I will praise You with music, telling of Your faithfulness to all Your promises.
    —Psalm 71:22, 23

Charles A. Miles
Arr. Mary K. Sallee

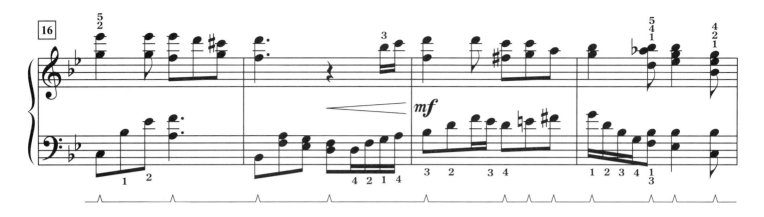

Allargando

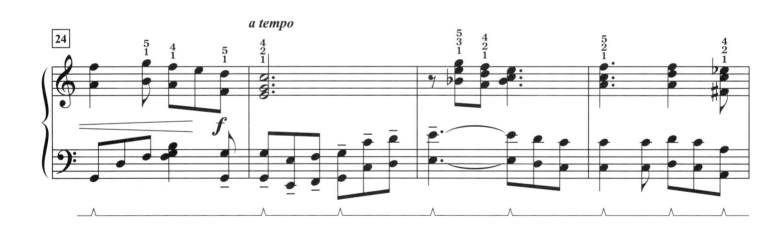

a tempo

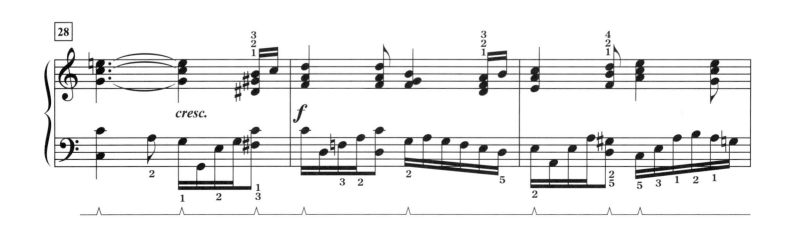

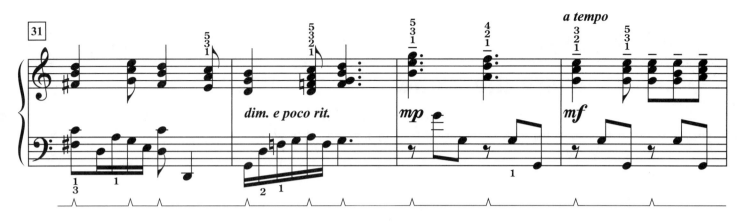

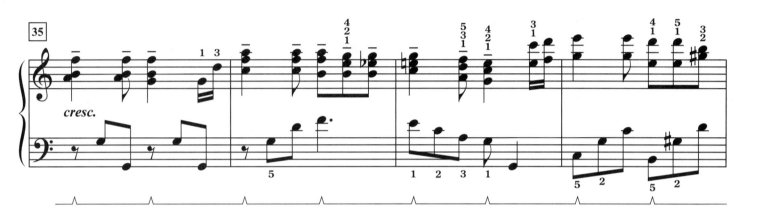

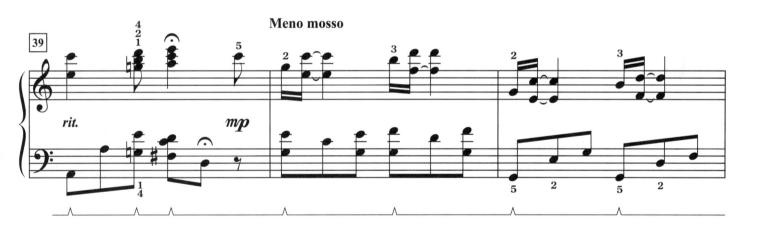

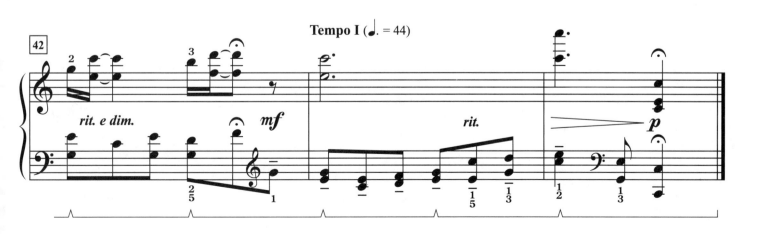

THE CROSS, CHRIST'S PASSION

I. When I Survey the Wondrous Cross

May I never boast except in the cross of our Lord Jesus Christ,
through which the world has been crucified to me, and I to the world.
   —Galations 6:14

Lowell Mason
Arr. Mark Hayes

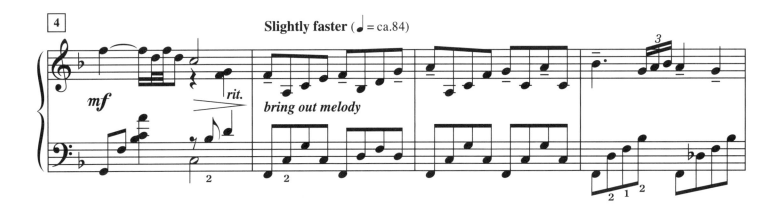

II. O Sacred Head, Now Wounded

The soldiers twisted together a crown of thorns and put it on his head.
    —John 19:2

Hans Leo Hassler
Harmonized by J. S. Bach
Arr. Mark Hayes

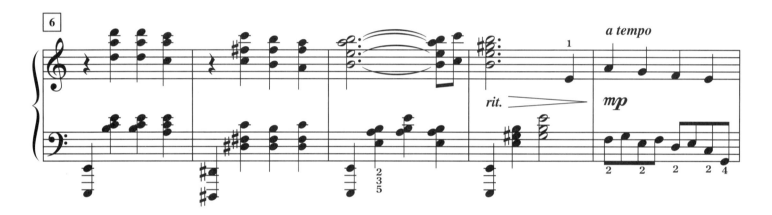

III. What Wondrous Love Is This?

But God demonstrates His own love for us in this: While we were still sinners, Christ died for us.
   —Romans 5:8

Traditional
Arr. Mark Hayes

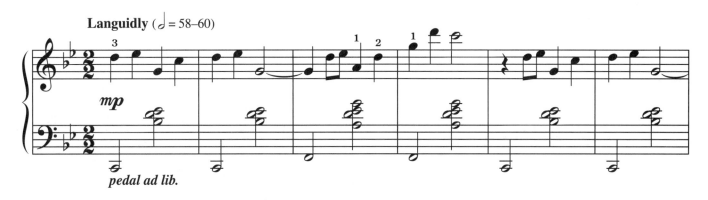

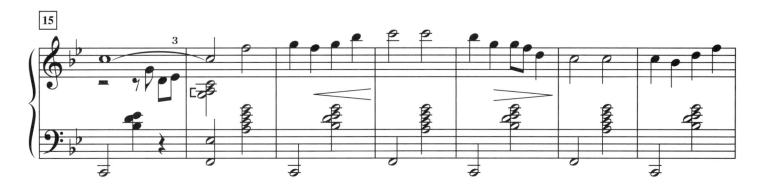

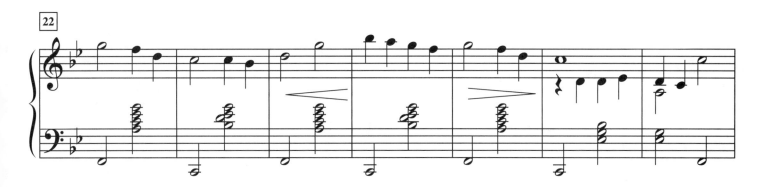

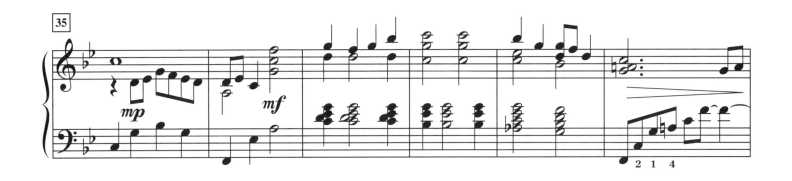

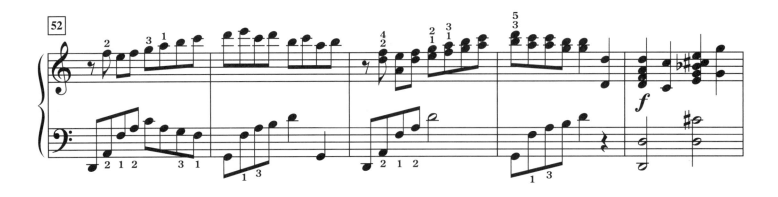

WORSHIP CHRIST THE KING

I. Holy, Holy, Holy

Holy, holy, holy, is the Lord of hosts: the whole earth is full of His glory.
—Isaiah 6:3

John B. Dykes
Arr. Kenon D. Renfrow

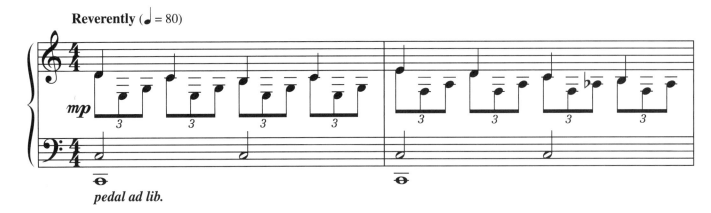

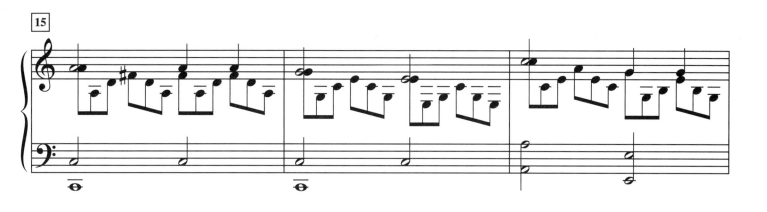

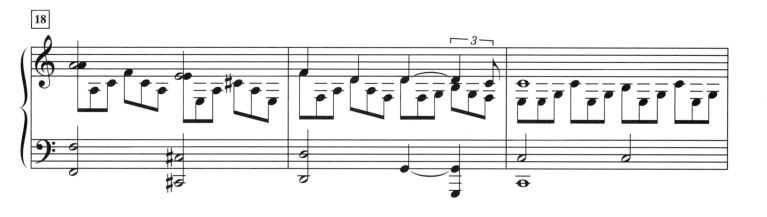

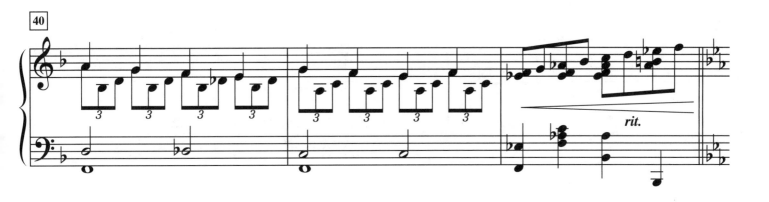

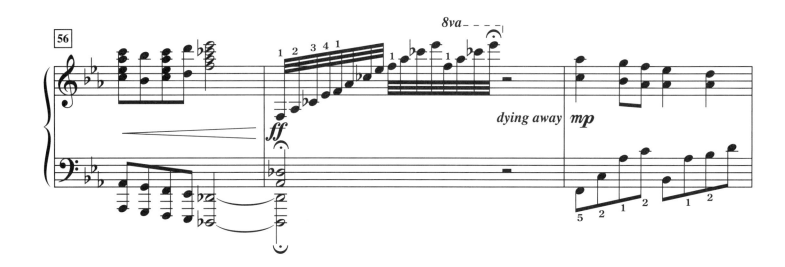

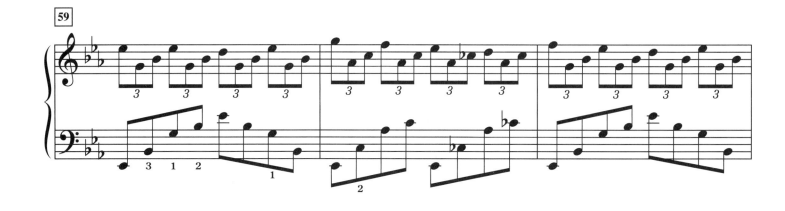

II. O Worship the King

Worship the King, the Lord of hosts.
  —Zechariah 14:16

Johann Michael Haydn
Arr. Kenon D. Renfrow

114

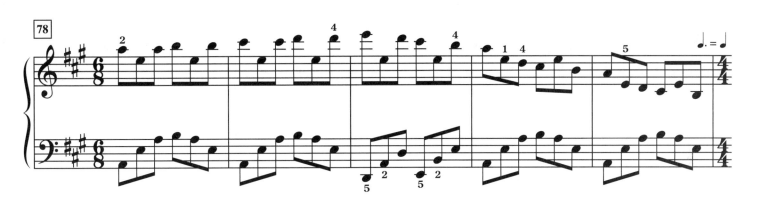

III. When Morning Gilds the Skies

My voice shalt Thou hear in the morning, O Lord.
    —Psalm 5:3

Josephy Barnby
Arr. Kenon D. Renfrow

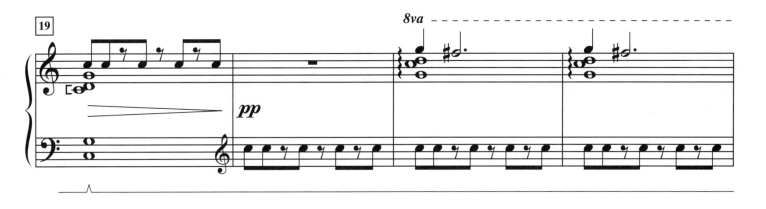

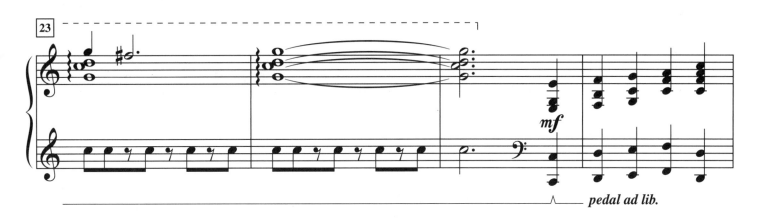

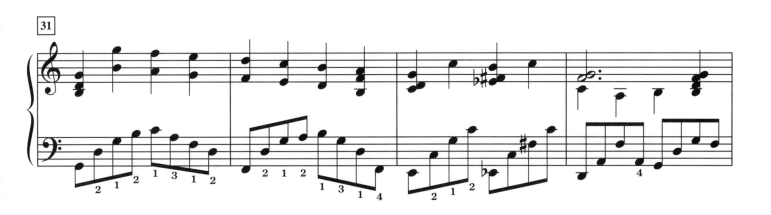

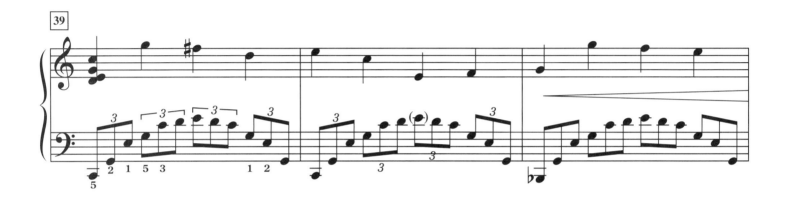

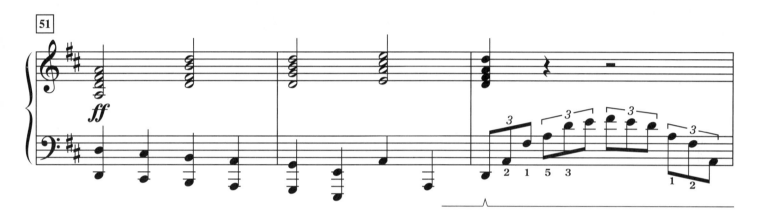

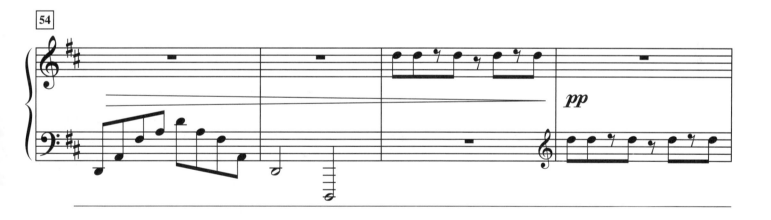

TRUST IN HIM

I. Trust and Obey

Let him trust in the name of the Lord and rely upon his God.
—Isaiah 50:10

Daniel B. Towner
Arr. Larry Dalton

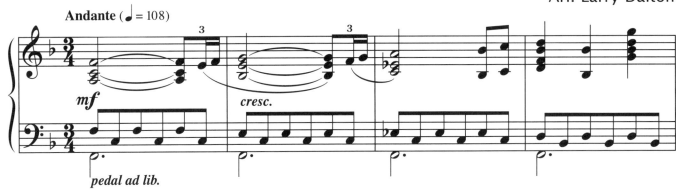

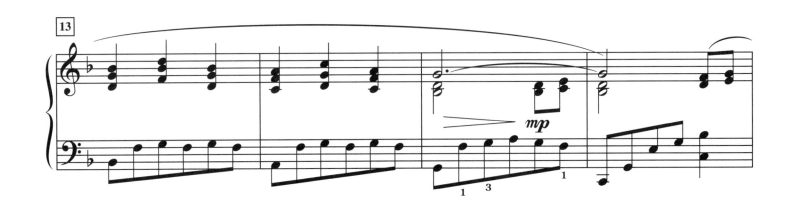

II. Only Trust Him

Trust in the Lord with all thine heart,
and lean not to thine own understanding.
      —Proverbs 3:5

John H. Stockton
Arr. Larry Dalton

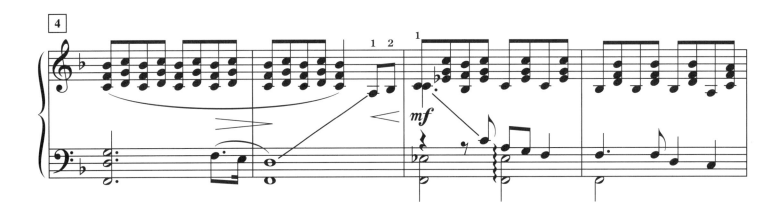

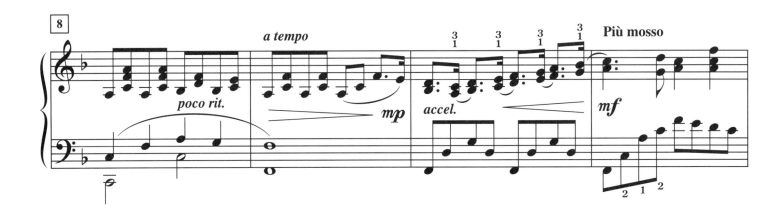

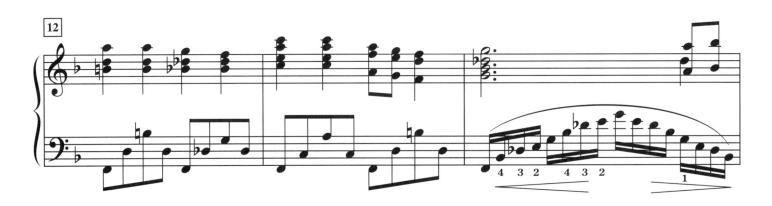

III. My Hope Is Built

For You are my hope, O Lord God; You are my trust from my youth.
—Psalm 71:5

William B. Bradbury
Arr. Larry Dalton

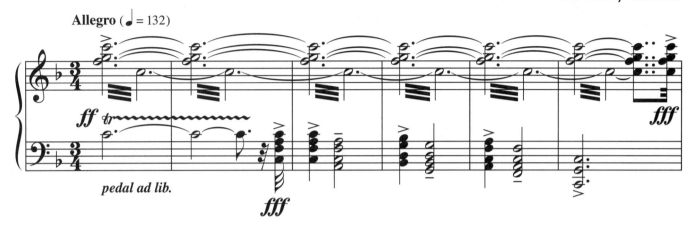

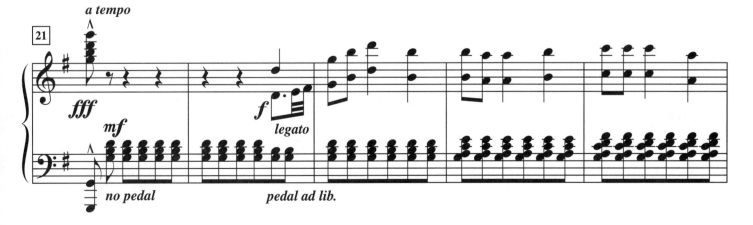

* Small note is optional.

SHARING THE GOOD NEWS

I. Jesus Shall Reign

All kings will bow down to Him and all nations will serve Him.

—Psalm 72:11

John Hatton

Arr. Matt Hyzer

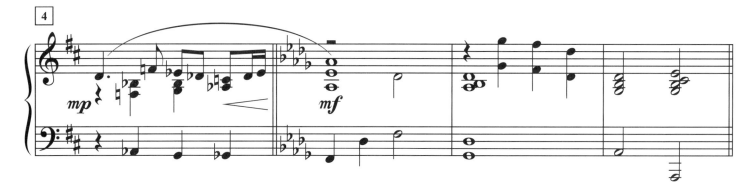

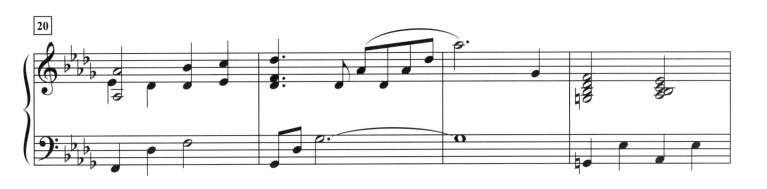

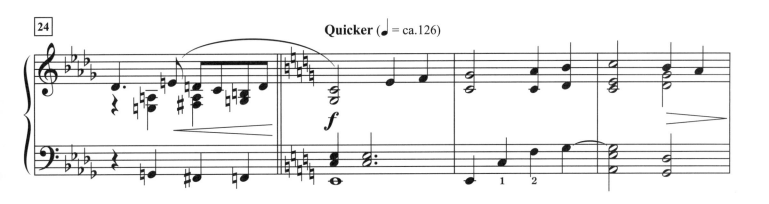

II. Rescue the Perishing

The Son of Man came to seek and to save what was lost.
  —Luke 19:10

William H. Doane
Arr. Matt Hyzer

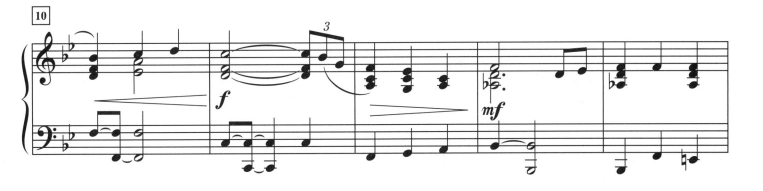

* Small notes are optional.

III. O Zion, Haste

Go into all the world and preach the good news to all creation.
—Mark 16:15

James Walch
Arr. Matt Hyzer

GOD, OUR CREATOR

I. I Sing the Mighty Power of God

For in six days the Lord made the heavens and the earth,
the sea, and all that is in them.

Gesangbuch der Herzogel, Wirtembergischen
Katholischen Hofkapelle
Arr. Anna Laura Page

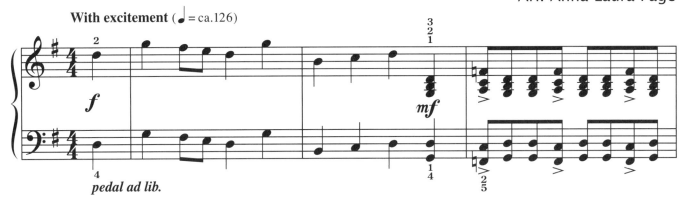

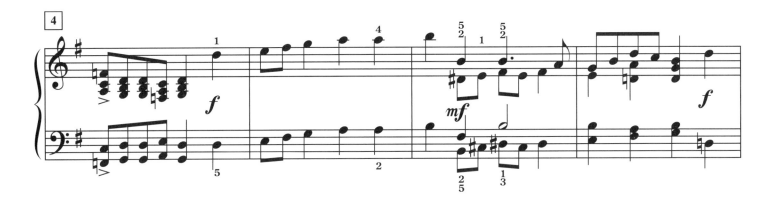

* "Old Hundredth," Genevan Psalter

II. This Is My Father's World

You are worthy, O Lord, to receive glory and honor and power; for
You created all things, and by Your will they exist and were created.
  —Revelation 4:11

Franklin L. Sheppard
Arr. Anna Laura Page

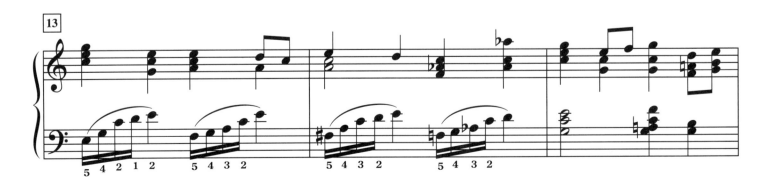

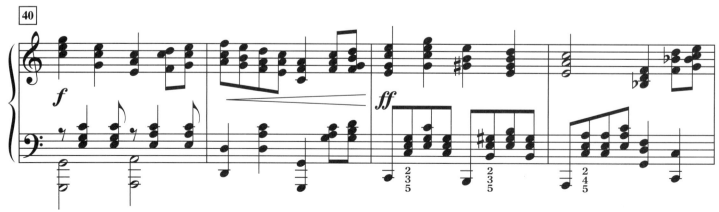

* "He's Got the Whole World in His Hands," Traditional

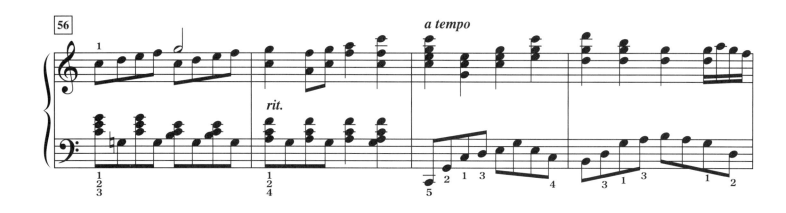

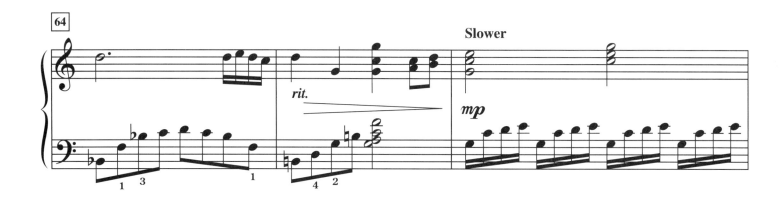

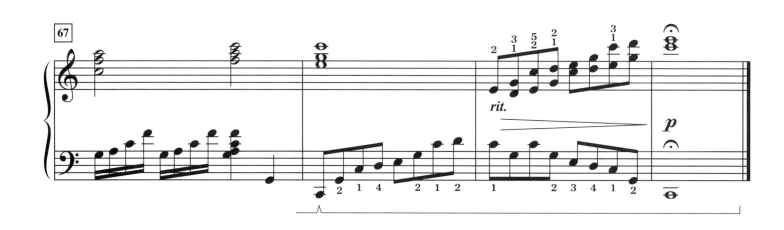

III. All Things Bright and Beautiful

He has made everything beautiful in its time.
    —Ecclesiastes 3:11

I will praise you, O God, with my whole heart; I will tell of all Your marvelous works.
    —Psalm 9:1

17th–century English Melody
Arr. Anna Laura Page

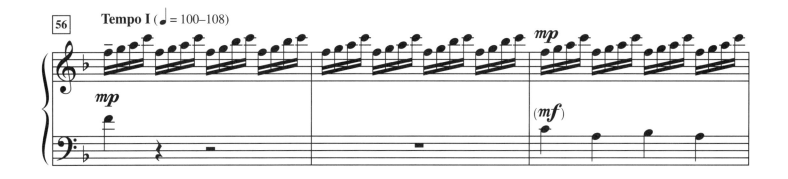

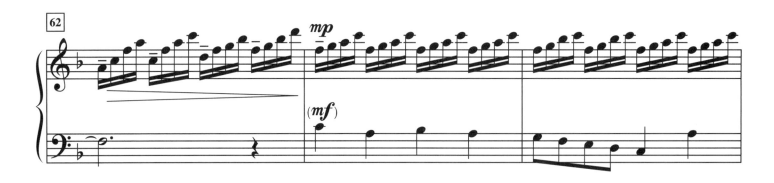

CONSECRATION

I. Take My Life and Let It Be

Surely goodness and mercy shall follow me all the days of my life,
and I shall dwell in the house of the Lord forever.
  —Psalm 23:6

Henri A. C. Malan
Arr. Larry Dalton

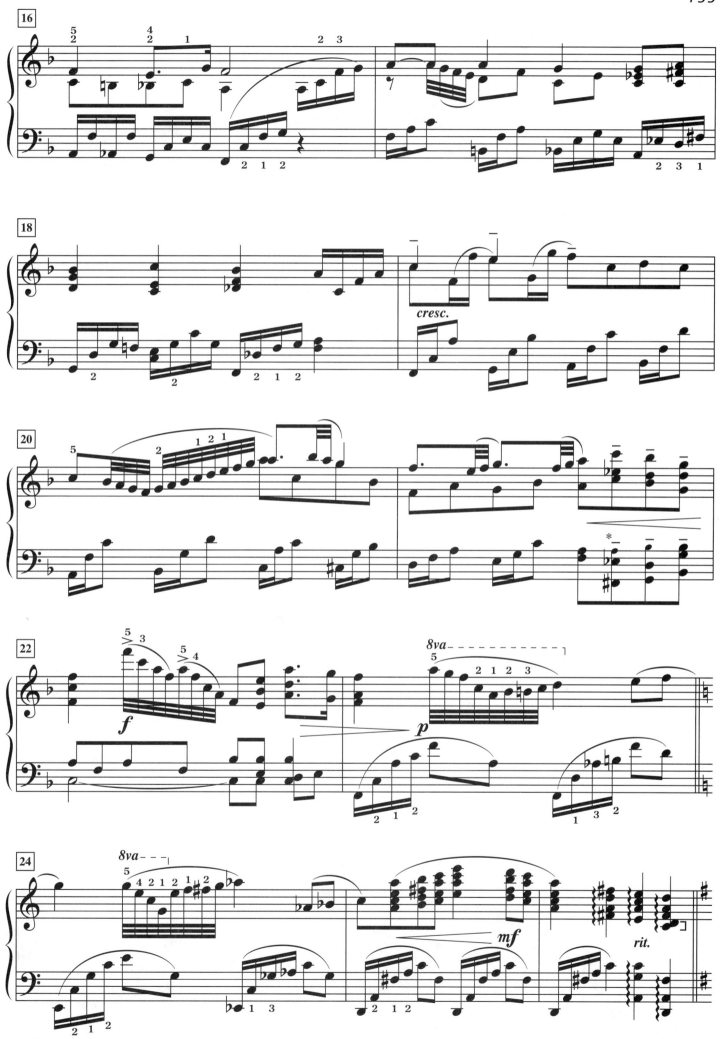

* All small notes are optional.

II. I Am Thine, O Lord

For whoever desires to save his life will lose it, but whoever loses his life for My sake will find it.
—Matthew 16:25

William Howard Doane
Arr. Larry Dalton

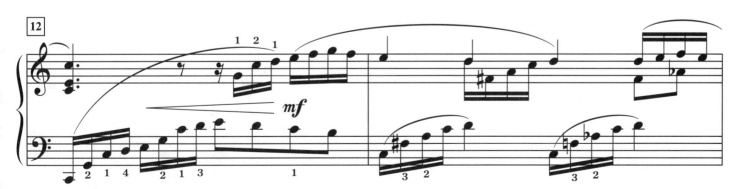

* All small notes are optional.

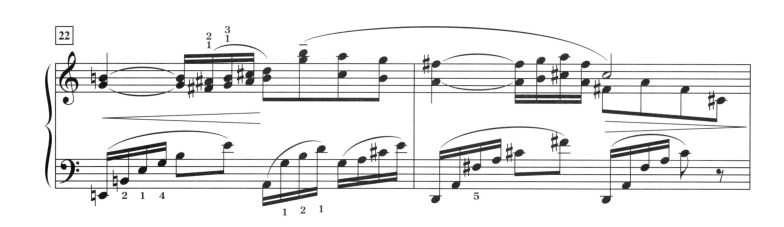

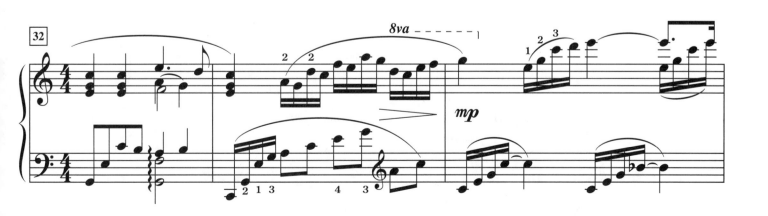

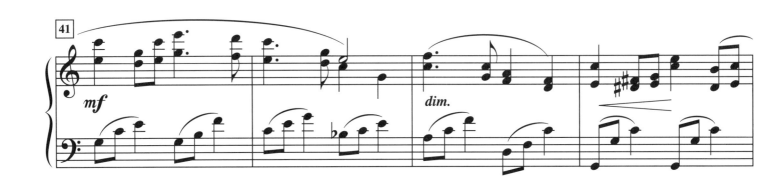

III. I'll Go Where You Want Me to Go

Master, I will follow Thee whithersoever Thou goest.
   —Matthew 8:19

Carrie E. Rounsefell
Arr. Larry Dalton

THE TRINITY

I. Eternal Father, Strong to Save

Save me, O God, by Thy Name, and judge me by Thy strength.
—Psalm 54:1

John B. Dykes
Arr. Myra Schubert

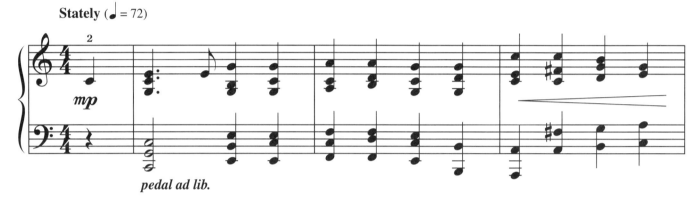

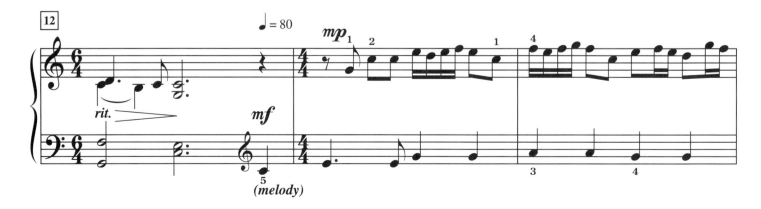

II. Jesus, the Very Thought of Thee

And Jesus, crying out with a loud voice, said, "Father, into Thy hands
I commit My spirit." And having said this, He breathed His last.
  —Luke 23:46

John B. Dykes
Arr. Myra Schubert

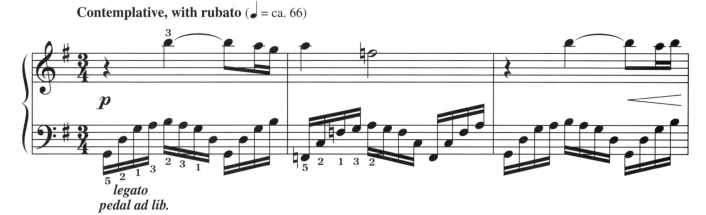

III. O Spirit of the Living God

"And it shall be in the last days," God says, "that I will pour forth of My Spirit upon all mankind; and your sons and your daughters shall prophesy, and your young men shall see visions, and your old men shall dream dreams."
—Acts 2:17

Traditional English Melody
Arr. Myra Schubert

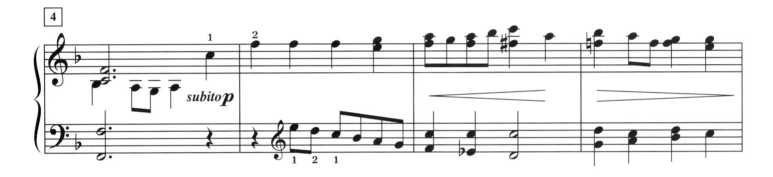

THE WORD OF GOD

I. Break Thou the Bread of Life

And the very words I have spoken to you are spirit and life.
—John 6:63

William F. Sherwin
Arr. Bernadine Johnson

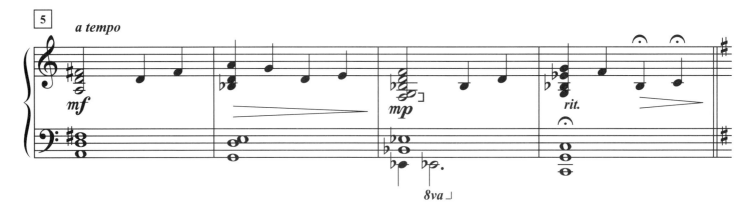

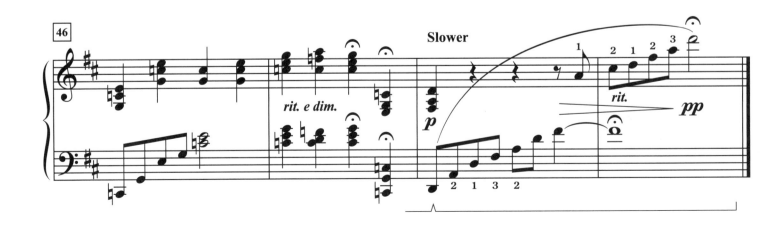

II. Holy Bible, Book Divine

Every word of God proves true.
    —Proverbs 30:5

William B. Bradbury
Arr. Bernadine Johnson

III. Standing on the Promises

So make every effort to apply the benefits of these promises to your life.
—II Peter 1:15

R. Kelso Carter
Arr. Bernadine Johnson

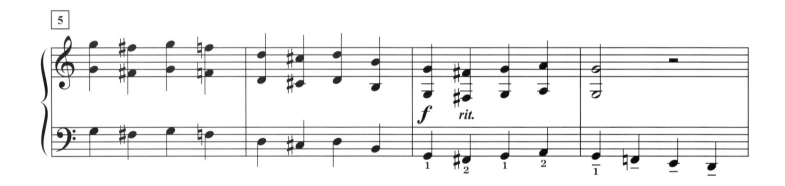

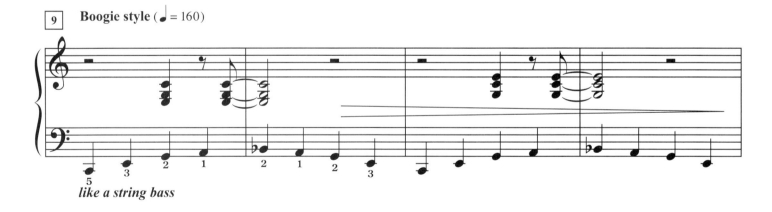

GOD'S LOVE

I. Jesus Loves Me

I will sing of the lovingkindness of the Lord forever.
—Psalm 89:1

William B. Bradbury
Arr. Shirley Brendlinger

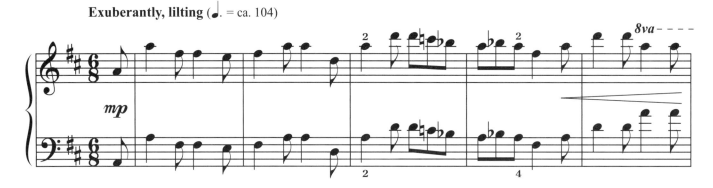

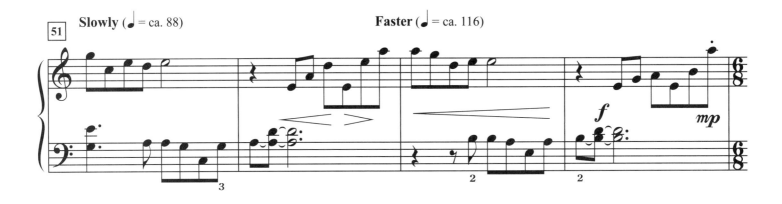

II. What Wondrous Love Is This?

For God so loved the world that He gave His only begotten Son...
—John 3:16

William Walker
Arr. Shirley Brendlinger

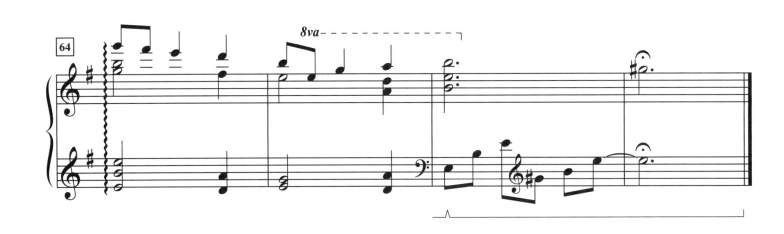

III. Of the Father's Love Begotten

*"I am the Alpha and the Omega,"says the Lord God, "who
is and who was and who is to come, the Almighty."*
—Revelation 1:8

13th-century Plainsong
Arr. Shirley Brendlinger

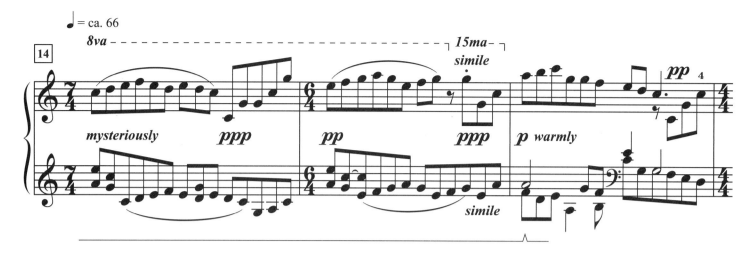

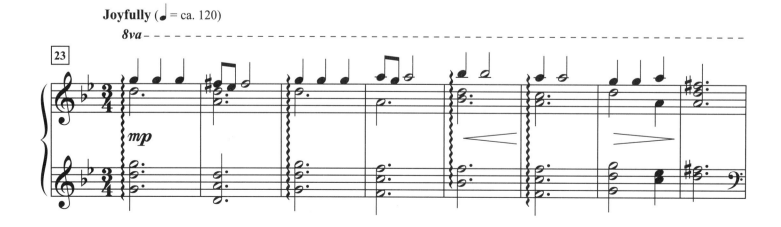

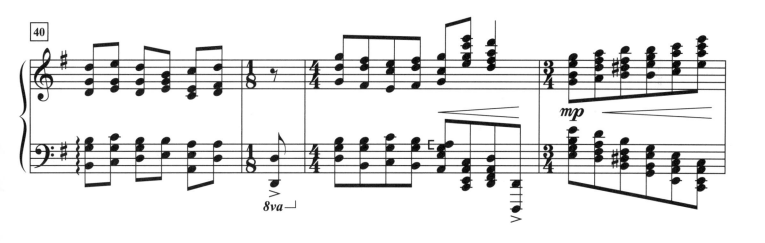